To Desiree

Never be afraid to do what you have been called to. Discover your gifts & share them with the world. The world needs what you have to offer!

Love Nancy

LIVE ON PURPOSE

A GUIDE ON HOW TO LIVE A PURPOSEFUL AND EMPOWERED LIFE

Nancy Arroyo Ruffin

Founder, The FIERCE Woman™

Live On Purpose is published by
CreativeINK Publishing
Bergenfield, NJ 07621
info@nancyarroyoruffin.com

Cover Design and Concept by
Sal Acosta
s.artist22@yahoo.com
917.774.1320

ISBN: 0692552146

ISBN-13: 978-0692552148

DEDICATION

For my girls, Avarie & Alexah, who have taught me what it means to live life purposely, intentionally, and passionately.

CONTENTS

ACKNOWLEDGEMENTS

This book developed organically as a result of my life experiences within the last five years. During that time I've given birth to two beautiful girls, written three books, and founded a women's empowerment organization. All of which would have never materialized had I not done some serious self-work. The journey has not been easy, but it has definitely been worth it. Along the way I've met amazing women, who through their own work, have shown me the importance of living an authentic life, following your heart, and committing to the process. Self-discovery is never easy, but if you do the work the benefits are worth it. Thank you to my mentor and spiritual teacher *Gloria Rodriguez*, who through her organization, the DeAlmas Women's Institute helped me to realize and discover my purpose in life. Thank you to my husband *Lamar Ruffin* for never doubting me and allowing me to spread my wings and fly. Thank you to my daughters who are my biggest inspirations. Thank you to my parents *Daniel & Margarita Arroyo* for instilling in me the importance of hard work and self-love. To my sister *Diana*, brother *Johanny*, nieces *Marissa* & *Danielle*, and my nephew *JD* thank you for always having my back. I love and appreciate you all more than you can ever know. Thank you to my in laws *Ron & Ann Ruffin* for all you do for our family. Your help with the girls means everything. Thank you to my *Titi Millie* for showing me what it really means to be a FIERCE woman. To my rider and partner in creative rebellion *Maria Rodriguez*, thank you for your unwavering support and always on time words of encouragement. Grateful for our bond, sis. Thank you to my soul brother *Gerald Medina* for all the laughs, talks, and moments of inspiration that result from just being around each other. And lastly, thank you to all my FIERCE women, it is because of you I do what I do. Never stop dreaming. Never stop pushing. Never stop believing in your power. This book is for you.

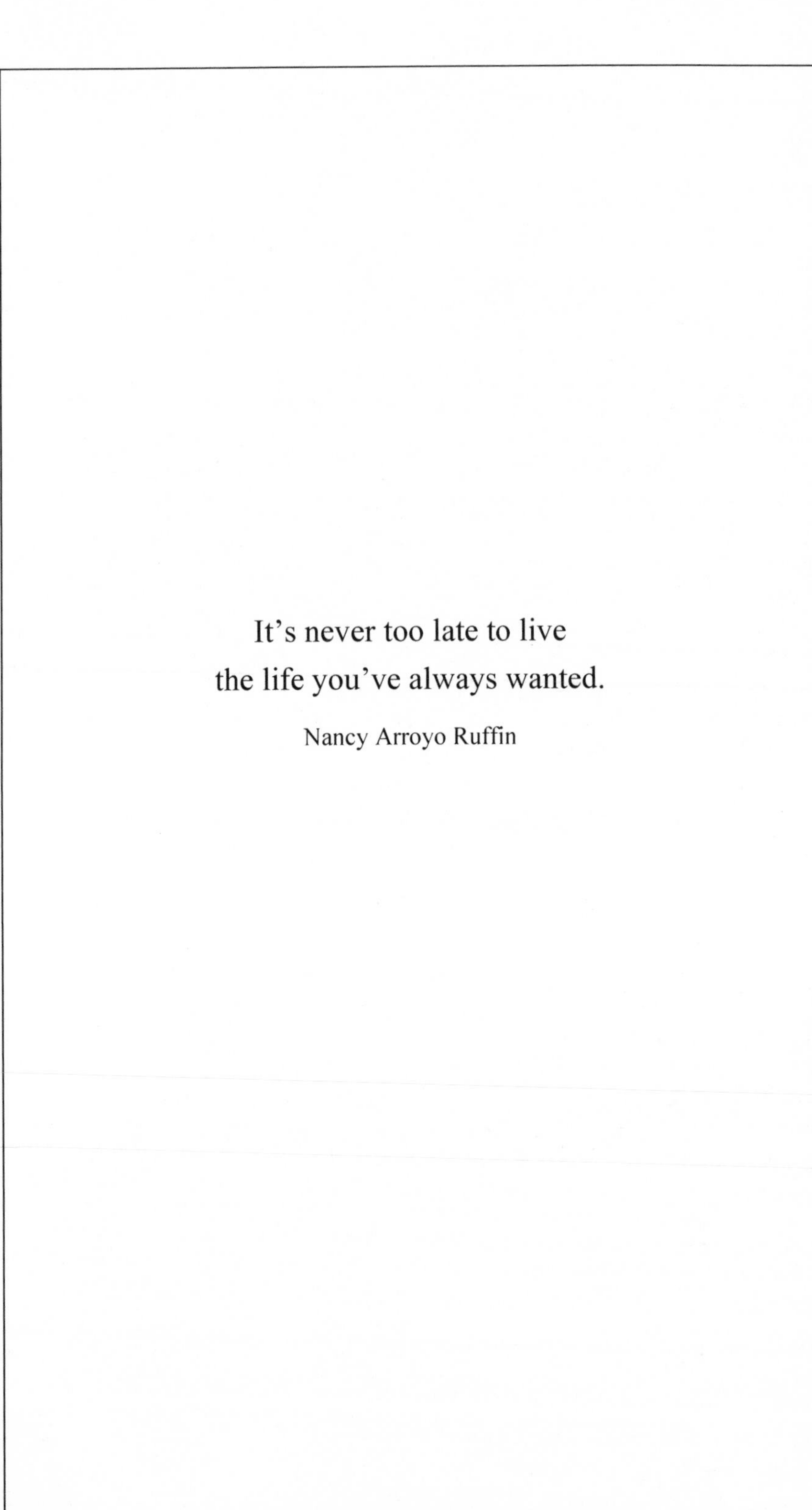

It’s never too late to live
the life you’ve always wanted.

Nancy Arroyo Ruffin

1

LIVING ON PURPOSE

"Your purpose in life is to find your purpose and give your whole heart and soul to it."
— Gautama Buddha

Why am I here? What am I supposed to do with my life? How many of us have asked ourselves these very questions or some variation of them throughout our lives? From as early as kindergarten we are asked by our teachers, our parents, even family members *what do you want to be when you grow up*?

At the ages of five and six our answers are simple. They are usually centered around what we've been exposed to at the time. Some may answer teacher, doctor, or police officer. Others may aspire to follow in the footsteps of their parents or care givers.

Whatever the answer is at age five, it is likely to change the older one gets.

As we get older and become more aware of our talents and things we enjoy, what we aspire to changes. We may still want to be a teacher, doctor, or police officer, but now that decision is based on our own personal desires, ambitions, and goals. Often times what we choose as a career has very little to do with our *purpose*.

There were many things I wanted to be when I was a kid. They varied from being a news journalist to becoming the first female President of the United States. Even as a child I had ambitious dreams. However, what I decided on once I entered college had little to do with what I was passionate about and more to do with stability and security. As per my dad, I needed to secure a good job so I would never have to depend on a man to take care of me.

Though I had no clue what I wanted to do with my life, I decided to major in Accounting. I wasn't very good with numbers and hated math, but accounting was a good profession and one in which I could earn a decent living. My mother had worked various administrative jobs while my father spent many years working in retail.

As the manager of a men's shoe store he was often required to work holidays and weekends. His busy work schedule limited the time he spent with me and my sister. This was one of the reasons that ensuring we went to college was a big deal to them. They didn't want us to settle. They wanted us to have choices.

My parents, both whose highest level of formal education is a high school diploma, firmly believed having a college education would open doors for us that were closed to them. They believed, and still do, that education is the key to our future. For them, having a degree equals freedom; freedom to choose the type of jobs we want and never having to settle doing work we didn't want to do in order to make ends meet. They wanted my sister and I to be independent women and getting an education would make that possible.

Despite my disdain for numbers and math I eventually earned my undergraduate degree in accounting. And while having the degree has given me many opportunities and opened many doors, I am not using the accounting degree for the purpose it was intended. I am not now nor have I ever worked as an accountant. That accounting degree is sitting on my wall and collecting dust while the interest on my student loans accrues.

Accounting was never my dream. It is not what I am passionate about and it isn't what sets my soul on fire. What sets my soul on fire is being able to help others discover their purpose and achieve their dreams. It wasn't until the birth of my oldest daughter in 2011 that I realized what my purpose in this life is. If you haven't discovered your purpose yet, don't get discouraged. You still have time.

WHAT IS PURPOSE?

How does one discover what their purpose is and more importantly what does one do once they've identified it? On an intellectual level, purpose is the reason for which something is done or created or for which something exists. On a spiritual level, purpose is the reason why you were created by God, Yahweh, Jehovah, Allah, the Universe, or whatever name you use to identify with the higher spiritual source (for the purpose of this book I will be using God and the Universe interchangeably). It is the reason you were placed on this planet. In short, it is the reason you exist.

Though many tend to describe themselves by their careers and job titles you are not your job. You are not your career, or your accomplishments, or what you do. If you were to suddenly lose any of those things, at your core, you would still be you. You do not stop being who you are because you suddenly find yourself on an unemployment line.

In his book, *The Purpose Driven Life*, author Rick Warren says “The purpose of your life is far greater than your own personal fulfillment, your peace of mind, or even your happiness. It’s far greater than your family, your career, or even your wildest dreams and ambitions.” Therefore, if purpose isn’t about your own desires and personal fulfillment what exactly is it?

Every object, thing, product that has ever been created has a purpose. Including you. Consider a baseball bat. Though it can be used for many things, its purpose is to hit baseballs. That's what it was created to do. Now imagine the baseball bat sits in the closet or in the trunk of your car and never gets used. Months go by and no one notices or even pays attention to the baseball bat. The baseball bat doesn't care because it is an inanimate object. It doesn’t have the ability to think or to feel or to reason.

However, imagine that same baseball bat with a soul, a spirit, a self-consciousness. Pretend her name is Betty. Days and months go by and Betty the baseball bat remains in the closet without anyone using her, without anyone touching her or acknowledging her. Suddenly she begins wondering why she isn’t being used.

Betty knows something is not quite right, but she doesn't know what it is. She begins questioning her purpose because she has no idea who she is or what it is she should be doing. Maybe you’ve felt the same way once in your life. Maybe you've become accustomed to "going with the flow" and are floating through life taking it day by day with no clear direction because you have not discovered what your purpose is.

Then one day someone decides to pull Betty out of the closet. They use her to break a car window because they've locked their keys in the car. Betty is overjoyed because she's finally being used; being held, being swung, smashing the window into fragments —Betty loves it. At the end of the day, though, she is still unfulfilled. Hitting the window and smashing it to pieces was exhilarating, but it wasn't enough. Something is still missing.

In the weeks that follow Betty is used often, but not for the purpose that she was created. Though Betty is no longer sitting idle in the closet she still feels empty. She yearns for more action, more fulfillment. She wants to be used as much as possible to knock things around, to hit things, to be held and to be swung. She surmises that she just hasn't had enough of these events to gratify her. She believes that she needs to be used more in order to feel more fulfilled.

Then one day little Alex pulls Betty out of the closet, takes her out to the ballpark, and uses her to hit a baseball. Suddenly, a spark within her is ignited. The smacking sound of the ball against her wood finish makes her baseball bat soul come alive. She feels a burst of joy and excitement she's never felt before. She now realizes what she was truly designed for. She was meant to hit baseballs. All the other things she hit in the past pale in comparison.

She now comprehends what her baseball bat soul was searching for all along. It was searching for its purpose. We all long for that aha! moment when our souls come alive and we finally realize what we were created for. We are like Betty longing to come alive. We know something is missing, but don't know what will end the emptiness and lack of fulfillment in our lives. And until we discover our purpose our souls won't ever truly come alive. No one wants to float through life. Yet many of us do because we do not know what our purpose is.

I hated almost every minute of undergrad school working towards that expensive accounting degree. I stuck through it because at the time I believed having a "good" job would make me happy. I now know that isn't true. If you don't love what you do, you will never be happy. Read that sentence again.

> *If you don't love what you do, you will never be happy.*

You will wake up every day miserable and unfulfilled. The greatest gift you can ever give yourself is to discover what your purpose is and then spend every day of your life fulfilling it.

BELIEVE IN YOUR MAGIC

We are all born with magic inside of us. As children we are carefree, rambunctious, curious, and fearless. We believe we can be anything we want to be. As we get older and are exposed to different people and begin having different experiences we start losing some of those qualities.

We begin to believe the lies society and the media tells us about ourselves. We begin to doubt ourselves. We believe we are not good enough, not deserving enough, not worthy enough. We convince ourselves our dreams are impossible and not worth pursuing and so we take less risks. We get comfortable with the familiar and the mundane and learn to be satisfied with mediocrity.

Somewhere along the line we forget who we are and we lose our spark, our magic. Poet, Peggy Robles-Alvarado says it best, "*magic making is not for pendejas*."

To believe in one's own magic is to go against everything society has taught us to believe about ourselves; that we are not worthy, not special enough, not important enough, not good enough. We have been conditioned to believe playing it safe is more important than taking risks, especially when it's on ourselves. We are taught to believe only a chosen few succeed. The reality is we can all succeed if we only take a chance and never give up.

When I decided to write this book I knew I wanted to share with the rest of the world some of what I've learned these past five years of my life. I wasn't sure of the theme or even the topics I wanted to discuss, but I knew I wanted to help others take control of their destinies.

In 2010, after trying unsuccessfully for years to conceive, I decided I no longer wanted to merely be a passenger in my life's journey. I needed to hop in the driver's seat and take control. I decided if I wanted to become a mother my husband and I could no longer sit idle and wait for mother nature to do her thing. If I wanted to realize my motherhood dreams I would have to take control of the wheel and actively aid the process.

The journey to motherhood was not easy. There were countless visits to a fertility doctor and numerous intrauterine insemination cycles which always resulted in negative pregnancy tests. There were many nights where I was riddled with self-doubt and guilt. There were times where I felt like my heart was being ripped from my chest; times where I cursed God and myself for not being able to do what my body as a woman was meant to do. There were times when giving up felt easier than continuing on, but I'm no quitter and I knew quitting would not fill the empty hole in my heart.

It wasn't until I decided to stop playing the victim and started taking action of my God given powers as a creator that things started to change. I began believing in my magic. Change your thoughts, change your life. That was exactly what I did.

Instead of focusing on the fact I wasn't yet a mother, I began seeing myself as a mother. I started doing things I would do if I was pregnant. I stopped drinking. I started eating healthier and taking better care of my body. I began visualizing what being a mother felt and looked like. I made becoming a mother my central focus.

I created a vision board with images of babies, mothers, and healthy living. I placed it in my bedroom so that it was the first thing I saw upon waking up in the morning and the last thing I saw when I went to sleep. I started a journal and started writing letters to my unborn child. In essence, what I was doing was putting out into the universe my heart's deepest desire knowing and trusting that as long as I believed I was a mother my reality would soon catch up with my vision. You have to see and believe it in order to achieve it.

In May 2011 I became pregnant for the very first time in my life. My husband and I were thrilled. My dream had finally come true, or so I thought. During my 8wk prenatal visit the doctor could no longer detect the baby's heartbeat. He informed us that this wasn't a viable pregnancy and that I would miscarry. My heart shattered. A few days later my body confirmed what the doctor had said.

I sat in my bathroom heartbroken watching my body rid itself of my baby. So consumed with sadness, I vowed I wouldn't try again. I decided I could not bear to experience that kind of pain again. Now, while my mind was saying I was done, my heart was still empty and I still longed to be a mother. I could not ignore my heart's deepest desire so my husband and I decided to try again.

In November 2011, only five months after the anguish of the miscarriage, I learned I was pregnant again. Here I was, a woman who had never been pregnant before, with child for the second time in a year. All the maternal energy I was putting out into the world finally came to life on July 27, 2012 when I gave birth to a beautiful and healthy baby girl.

Though the journey was difficult and not at all how I envisioned conceiving my child, when your back is against the wall you can either stay there and allow yourself to be defeated or you can push back and fight. I chose to fight. What I learned during the process was exactly what Paulo Coelho says in his book, *The Alchemist,* "*When you want something, all the universe conspires in helping you achieve it.*"

Sometimes it is hard to pick up and start again when it seems like the cards are stacked against us. Being able to believe in something greater than ourselves requires a great deal of faith, but when faith is all that's left you have to be willing to let go and let God.

When following your dreams you will be tested. You will experience insurmountable odds and challenges that will test your will, your faith, and belief in yourself. It is often when one is closest to realizing their dream that they give up. I encourage you not to.

Instead, pay attention to every roadblock and challenge that presents itself. They show up for a reason. Reflect on the challenge and ask yourself what is the knowledge or insight you're supposed to uncover. Remember, every struggle holds a lesson within it and that struggle will continue to show up in different ways until you learn what it is trying to teach you.

> *Learn to get in touch with the silence within yourself and know that everything in this life has a purpose. There are no mistakes, no coincidences. All events are blessings given to us to learn from. - Elizabeth Kübler-Ross*

There is something you need to learn before you can continue on your journey. Be open to it and trust yourself enough to know you have the power within yourself to make the impossible, possible. Impossible is what we tell ourselves when we're afraid. Fear is such a powerful emotion that it can simply override all other feelings, logic or priorities. I'm here to tell you fear is a liar. Fear will wrap its arms around you and render you immobile if you let it. It will make you stagnant. We worry that our worst fears may come true so we don't take action. And ironically, exactly that which we fear is what we bring to life.

Conquering our fears begins with the acknowledgment that oftentimes fear is a decision, not an inherent trait or needed component of life. Once you make the decision to push passed the fear you are well on your way to conquering them. Face what scares you head-on, and challenge your trepidation. The worse thing that can happen when chasing your dreams is that you fail. So what. Failure is a stepping stone to success. Everyone who has ever accomplished anything great has failed at one time. Do not allow the fear of failure prevent you from acting.

Just START. Start wherever you are with whatever you have. Do something, anything. Even if it's just getting out of bed (I've been there many times), opening a word document and writing one line, or asking someone for help. Once you face your fears you dreams become limitless.

I am writing this book as a testament to the wonderful things that can happen when you realize your purpose. I am writing this book to help you reclaim your magic; to help you realize just how great, worthy, and deserving you are to live the life you've always imagined for yourself. My hope is that you reconnect with your source and change your self-concept. What you believe yourself to be is what you become. Repeat that sentence to yourself.

What I believe to be, I become.

Whoever you are or whatever it is that you want, when you really want something it's because that desire was created in you. God would not put a dream in your heart without also giving you the tools, skills, and wisdom necessary to make it come true.

You can hide from your dream and pretend it doesn't exist. You can bury it in the back of your mind and force yourself not to think about it, but until you acknowledge it you will spend your days on Earth floating through life. You will feel as if something is missing. You will be like Betty the baseball bat sitting in the closet waiting to be used. Don't wait. The time is now. Take action and start living on purpose. How do you do that? You start by reconnecting with the source.

Questions to ponder: 

Am I living a purposeful life? Am I making every day, hour, minute, second count? How can I live more intentionally? If someone asked me what my life's purpose is what would I tell them?

Use the space on the following pages to jot down any thoughts, phrases, or insights gained from the questions. The goal is to begin to dig deep within yourself and begin your journey of self-discovery. Beginning a meditation practice and daily journal writing can also aid in the self-discovery process.

2

RECONNECTING WITH THE SOURCE

"Get up in the morning and invite good things into your life" – Joel Osteen

---

When I lived in Brooklyn back in the 80s my sister and I would go to church every Sunday on our own. There was no coaxing or urging by our parents. It was something we loved to do. We'd attend the noon mass. We'd sit in the front pew and diligently listen to Father John deliver his homily and eagerly wait to receive communion. We did this for years. Our family was not very religious, but I was baptized in a Catholic Church and I was taught to believe in God.

When I lived in Brooklyn I spent a lot of time participating in church sponsored activities. It was a time where I was very connected to God. Growing up in a low-income, underserved community our local church had a free after school program where neighborhood kids could go to do homework, play, or just stay out of trouble. My sister and I went there every afternoon.

When Christmas came along they'd give presents to all the children in the program. Many came from single parent households and sometimes the gifts they received from the church where the only gifts they got.

During summer and holiday breaks Father John would take a group of kids to his house in Monticello, NY. It was the first time I'd experienced walking through the woods, and swimming in a lake. The property included a barn house and acres of land where we could run and play. There was a tree house and a huge field where we would play softball and dodgeball. For Halloween we'd dress up as Indians, paint our faces, and have a bonfire. At night we'd camp out under the moon and tell scary stories about Jeremiah Johnson. Being there felt safe. It was the exact opposite of the chalk and grit of my everyday Brooklyn life. I have many fond memories of this time in my life. I know the church, despite its flaws, definitely helped many of the kids stay off the streets and out of trouble.

When my parents decided to purchase a home some years later and we moved to Queens I stopped attending church. Now a teenager living in a new environment, I no longer felt the connection with God and the church I once did. For a long time after, I had virtually no relationship with God. Though I still believed in God and a higher spiritual being I somehow allowed myself to disconnect from my source. It wasn't until I decided to get married and needed to do my confirmation in order to have a church ceremony that I reconnected with God. Even then the connection wasn't genuine. It was merely a means to an end.

I got married August 2001 and after the ceremony I abandoned God and the church once again. I got what I wanted and didn't feel like I needed to re-establish my relationship with God. I was wrong. Though my wedding was absolutely beautiful, my marriage on the other hand was a complete mess. I was young, spoiled, and not ready for the commitment and compromise that marriage required. Without having God as the central force of our relationship my husband and I had no clear direction on how to make our marriage work.

We spent the first few years lost. We disrespected ourselves and our union. We continued to live separate lives and were very unhappy most of the time. We separated at least a dozen times and despite the many times we got back together and vowed to make things work, we didn't know how. We did not know how to merge our two lives into one. We didn't know how to let go of our old single lives and build a strong foundation that would allow our marriage to thrive. It's a struggle I believe many young newlyweds encounter.

I was 23 years old when I got married. I wasn't taught to be a wife. I was encouraged to go to school and start a career. I didn't know what being a wife in the new millennium meant. I was not June Cleaver. I saw myself more as Claire Huxtable, a successful career woman who had it all. Yet, real life was not as easy as they made it appear on TV. Most of the time I felt like I was stuck in a repeat episode of The Twilight Zone. I felt like a stranger in my own life.

It didn't take long before we decided we needed to seek professional help if we wanted our marriage to work. At first, we attended a marital retreat sponsored by the Catholic church for couples whose marriages were in trouble. When that didn't work we attended marriage counseling. Our counseling sessions often ended badly. Usually my husband would leave the session angrier than he'd been when it began. It wasn't until he was diagnosed with stage two Non-Hodgkin's Lymphoma in the winter of 2003 that we finally realized we needed to get serious about taking control of our marriage and actively work to fix it.

God has a way of slapping you in the face and making you realize what's important. Sometimes we get so lost and disconnected that it is only through tragedy or a life and death situation that we are able to get ourselves back on track.

God will give us plenty of chances and give us plenty of signs until we follow them. Until we learn to pay attention to the signs He will continue to put us through difficult and challenging situations. There is no easy way. The only way to change anything is to actively work towards changing it. This is true for every area of our lives. We are all capable at any time in our lives to change the direction of our life. We just have to make the decision to do so.

For my husband and I his cancer diagnoses was what we needed to get us back on track. His diagnoses brought us closer together. We understood that in order for him to beat this disease we needed to be unified. While he was busy fighting I was right by his side cheering him on and never allowing him to succumb to negative thoughts or feelings of despair. I like to think I was his rock and his strength on those days when the chemotherapy was too much or on the days when the pain was so unbearable that the only way he could find some relief was through the relief of his narcotics prescription.

Witnessing a loved one in so much pain doze in and out of consciousness while under the influence of narcotics, helped to put things in perspective for me. It made me realize I was not ready to lose my husband and although those where some very difficult times for the both of us, we got through them. Together. In the end he beat the cancer. Correction: WE beat the cancer. And our marriage was stronger than it had ever been.

My husband's determination and commitment to beat that disease was inspiring. He showed me, by his example, the miracles God can create when we just believe. He reconnected with his source and fought like hell to rid his body of the cancer that was trying to take over him. He was a warrior. He never felt sorry for himself. He didn't make excuses. He chose to fight. He chose to heal.

He used his God given strength to restore his health and rebuild his body. Yes, I'm sure the chemotherapy helped, but I firmly believe it was his sheer determination to not give up that helped him persevere. The moment he decided to fight and not surrender to this disgusting illness he chose to create a miracle. In doing so, he taught me that I too have the ability to create miracles and so do you.

When we start to see ourselves as all-powerful creative beings there is nothing we cannot accomplish.

Everything depends upon its attitude toward itself; that which it will not affirm as true of itself cannot awaken in this world. – Neville Goddard

There is a spark of God within you. You are made in God's image and as such have the power to manifest into your life all that your heart desires. In Dr. Wayne Dyer's book, *Wishes Fulfilled,* he speaks of this spark and how he believes this spark is our spiritual essence. He calls it the *highest self.*

He argues that as your awareness increases that you are a God-realized being, you will welcome it as the central focus of your life. In short, what he is saying is that not only do you have a spark of God within you, you in essence are God.

While that may be a revolutionary concept to understand and accept what its meant to convey is we cannot separate ourselves from our creator. He is you and you are Him. In the same way that you are a part of your mother and father they are too, a part of you. Therefore, since you are a manifestation of the almighty creator, you too are all-powerful and have the power to create miracles. This is your magic.

THE POWER OF I AM

Many of the world's prophets, seers, mystics, and spiritual leaders have discovered the power in the words I AM. They understand that anything that follows those 2 short, but very powerful words manifests into their reality.

When you say "I Am," you are announcing the Presence of God within you, as explained in the third chapter of Exodus. If you recall, the chapter begins with the revelation of God to Moses from a burning bush. It develops with God telling Moses to go back to

Egypt and deliver his people from their oppression and bondage. Moses unsure about how to accomplish such a task says to God,

> *"Who am I that I should go to Pharaoh and bring the Israelites out of Egypt?" God answered: I will be with you; and this will be your sign that I have sent you. When you have brought the people out of Egypt, you will serve God at this mountain. "But," said Moses to God, "if I go to the Israelites and say to them, 'The God of your ancestors has sent me to you,' and they ask me, 'What is his name?' what do I tell them?" God replied to Moses:* ***I am who I am****. Then he added: This is what you will tell the Israelites:* ***I AM*** *has sent me to you. God spoke further to Moses: This is what you will say to the Israelites: The LORD, the God of your ancestors, the God of Abraham, the God of Isaac, and the God of Jacob, has sent me to you.* ***This is my name forever; this is my title for all generations.***
>
> *–Exodus 3:12-15*

As you can see from this biblical passage "I Am" is how God identifies himself. Therefore, every time you say I Am you are affirming that you too are God. You are tapping into the God(dess) who resides within you. You must remember that your essence is the essence of God. It is your true being. It is your spirit, your soul, and yours only because no one else can say I Am for you. Only you can say "I Am".

You create your destiny and fate by the things which you attach to that I Am, for that is what you really believe yourself to be. Know who you are and *whose* you are. You are the perfect manifestation of God in human form.

For example, if you say to yourself, "I am afraid," then you are affirming and calling into your experience that which is based on fear. Every experience onward will be based on what you have affirmed for yourself. Do not allow fear to paralyze you. Do not allow fear to prevent you from going after what you want. Instead acknowledge the fear, feel the fear and do it anyway. Pushing through it is the only way to conquer it. It will be hard, it will be scary, it will be uncomfortable and there will be times when you'll feel like giving up, but keep going. Being fearless takes practice.

Your I AM-ness, your awareness, is how you transform your world. Whatever you attach to I Am you become. As you affirm with feeling, *I am fearless, inspired, motivated, loving, happy, peaceful, healthy and strong,* you will resurrect these qualities that may lie dormant within you, and miracles will happen in your life.

You must affirm who you are, what you want, and open yourself up daily to all the wonderful opportunities that are awaiting you. Your words become your reality. You must prophesize your future. Speak your dreams and desires into existence. Not only speak it, but envision it as if they have already come to pass. When you believe, it is only a matter of time before your reality catches up to your vision. Intention, awareness, momentum, and motivation creates miracles.

Questions to ponder: 

Are there any areas of my life where I am not being my authentic self? What behaviors or patterns prevent me from tapping into and connecting with my essence? How am I using "I AM" to manifest my dreams?

3

THE POWER OF *I AM*

"Be still, and know that I am God."
— Psalms 46:10 KJV

Joel Osteen wrote an entire book about the power of the words I Am. Essentially his book is about harnessing the power of words and using them to create your reality.

"Whatever follows the "I am" will eventually find you." — Joel Osteen

For me, I Am is more than two simple words. *I Am* is consciously acknowledging the God(dess) that exists in all of us. When we allow ourselves to harness the power of *I Am* that is when we are most attuned with our spirit. The bible says,

"Be still and know that I am God."
-Psalm 46-10

It is in stillness where I am able to connect with my true self. It is how I reconnect with my spirit. It is how I reconnect with the source. For the past five years I've been on an intentional journey of self-discovery and spiritual re-awakening.

This desire to reconnect with the source is magnetic. It's as if there is a cosmic force in the Universe pulling me, forcing me even, to dig deeper into myself. I cannot run from it. It is like my shadow, though I may not always see it I know it's there. It is constant and it is how I know there is more to my life than what I planned for it. God has a bigger plan for me, a bigger vision. It wasn't until I started meditating that the vision became clearer to me.

We bombard our brains with so much information, with so many visions, and so many ideas of who we want to be and what we want to do that we do not allow any space for God to reveal our purpose to us. Meditation allows us to clear our minds and be one with our creator. If prayer is defined as talking to God, then meditation is listening to the response. It is only through silence and stillness that one hears the voice of God.

If you're anything like I was you probably have no idea how to meditate. Or maybe you've tried it, but for whatever reason became frustrated, dismissed it as pointless and gave up. Meditation requires practice and the first few times you do it you may feel like you're doing it wrong. It's not as easy as it sounds to silence the chatter in your head. We have become so great at multi-tasking that our brains are always working.

We fill our lives with noise and in the midst of so much chaos it's no wonder many have turned away from the practice of meditation. We simply have not acquired the skills to quiet our minds long enough to reap any real benefit. The good news however, is the more you meditate the better you become at silencing the mind. You learn how to keep your thoughts at bay and learn how to listen to your inner voice, that which is the voice of your highest self, the voice of God.

In recent years, with the popularity of spiritual thought leaders like Dr. Wayne W. Dyer, Deepak Chopra, Joyce Meyer, Joel Osteen, Marianne Williamson, even Oprah Winfrey and the OWN Network's Super Soul Sunday programming more people are challenging themselves to live more purposeful and fulfilled lives. They are what I like to call, living intentionally. Many are craving a simpler way of life; challenging themselves to be more, to do more, and asking themselves how they can be more of service.

They are seeking a life where they can go back to basics and find a more intimate space with God without the many distractions which seem to clutter up our lives. A way to connect with the source in a manner which is pure and unhindered by the interruptions of our hectic, vociferous world.

There are many ways to connect with your spirit. Some connect best with their essence at church, while others connect better outdoors where they can be one with nature. Being outdoors in the woods or at the beach allows you to connect with God by reflecting on the beauty of what God has created. Hearing a bird sing or feeling the warmth of the sun penetrate your skin can have a calming and relaxing effect especially if all you're ever surrounded by is the congestion and noise found in busy metropolitan cities like Los Angeles, New York, or Chicago. While there is no perfect place for meditation it is ideal that wherever you choose is quiet, peaceful, and free of distraction.

CRASH COURSE ON MEDITATION

There have been many books and articles written on the practice of meditation. I will briefly share with you my meditation practice. What works for me is finding a quiet and peaceful place where the temperature is comfortable and the lighting is soft and warm. A place where I know I won't be disturbed by the sounds of a ringing telephone, or crying children, or the sound of the TV. Somewhere outdoors surrounded by nature is always nice, but this isn't always ideal especially if you live in a city like New York where noise and chaos seem to be everywhere.

I usually meditate in my home office which is on the second level of my home, away from everything. I enjoy lighting candles and sometimes I play meditation music to help me relax and still my mind. Once my spiritual space is ready I sit in a comfortable chair with my feet planted firmly on the ground or depending on how I feel, I sit Indian style on the floor.

I begin by taking deep slow breaths. I allow the oxygen to fill my lungs. Paying special attention to my breathing. Understanding that with each inhalation I am taking in confidence, joy, peace, trust, love, faith, patience. With each exhalation I am releasing all of the stress of the day. I am releasing negative and unproductive thoughts. I am releasing doubt, fear, anxiety, worry, self-loathing, anger and feelings of unworthiness.

I pay attention to any vibrations or energy in the room. I pay attention to how my body is responding. I pay attention to any changes in my breathing. Am I feeling more or less relaxed? Has my breathing changed? All of these things serve as cues because it is in these moments when you become in tune with the creator. You have to learn to pay attention to the signs, no matter how insignificant you think they may be. It is through these signs that spirit is talking to you.

When I was doing my self-work in 2011 with my spiritual mentor and founder of the DeAlmas Women's Institute, Gloria Rodriguez, it was through the practice of meditation that I was able to reconnect with spirit and God. It was during those moments of stillness where I discovered my purpose. It was where I realized my God given gift to create and nurture and be of service.

During one of my group sessions with Gloria and my fellow group members I expressed how frustrated I'd become on my journey to motherhood and that I wanted to give up. Through tears and sobs I told them I no longer believed I was meant to be a mother even though in my heart it was what I wanted most. They sat in silence and listened to me as I filled myself with words of self-doubt. When I was done speaking one of the ladies said to me,

> *"You have to trust that you are a mother. Have faith that it will happen. Believe that it will happen."*

That night I went home and meditated. I sat in silence for a long time. I waited for spirit to reveal itself to me. Tears welled up in my eyes and I allowed myself to cry. I released all of the self-doubt and negative energy I'd been carrying. I allowed myself to feel the pain attached with the tears. I allowed my spirit to cleanse itself. When I was done I opened up my journal and wrote the following:

> *Trust. Faith. Believe. These are the words I was gifted at tonight's group meeting. As I continue on this path of motherhood, tonight will be the last night I have any doubt. I will go to sleep tonight knowing I AM a mother. I will*

trust, have faith, and believe. This is my deepest desire and as I affirm it, it will be. This or something better.

At the time, I did not realize that by saying *I Am a mother* I was tapping into my magic and calling into my reality the vision I created for myself. I awoke the next morning feeling rejuvenated and brand new. I no longer felt the heaviness of the night before. I released my doubts and fears and woke up trusting, faithful, and believing. I woke up feeling like a mother.

A few weeks prior, I had completed an intrauterine insemination cycle. I walked into my bathroom that morning and at the nudging of my inner voice decided to take a pregnancy test. As I sat there waiting for the results I felt a bright light surround me. It was warm and welcoming. A vision of me holding a baby appeared. It was strong. I felt it as if I was actually holding the baby in my arms. It was the most bizarre an unexplainable experience I'd ever had. Yet, I allowed myself to trust the vision. All the self-work I'd done up to that point was preparing me for that moment. I knew before even looking at the test what the result was. I was pregnant. I was finally getting what I wanted most and all I needed to do was trust my own magic.

If you were to ask me what the most important experience of my life has been so far, I would say it was learning to meditate. Meditation has allowed me to connect with myself in a way that I never did before. It has changed the way I approach life and it has revealed to me my magic making capabilities. When we learn to listen, trust, and believe in ourselves we make miracles happen.

Questions to ponder:

How am I connecting with my spirit? What fears and doubts am I allowing to paralyze me? How can I use the power of I AM to change my thoughts, self-concept, and reality?

Take a few moments and complete the following:

I AM ________________________________

I AM ________________________________

I AM ________________________________

I AM ________________________________

Note: Only positive and self-affirming words should be placed after I Am

4

USING YOUR MAGIC TO CREATE MIRACLES

"Once you believe in yourself and see your soul as divine and precious, you'll automatically be converted to a being that can create miracles." —Wayne W. Dyer

---

Life doesn't just happen to us. We create our lives by the choices and decisions we make. Where you are right now in your life is a culmination of every thought, choice, and decision you've made up to this point. If you would have made a different choice in any area of your life it is likely that your current reality would have been altered by that decision.

While there are things that occur that are completely beyond our control, how we react is completely up to us. Our ability to reason and make decisions is what separates us from the rest of God's other creations. We do not have to float through life. We can choose at any time to live productive, fulfilled, and purposeful lives.

When my husband first learned of his cancer diagnoses he had two choices. He either could have resigned himself to the disease and given up or take his life into his own hands and resolve to fight a disease that claims thousands of lives every year. He chose the latter knowing that it would not be easy, but it would be worth it. He was not ready to give up on life or himself. He knew he had within him the strength, determination, and resolve to beat this disease.

Though his treatment was vigorous and required him to be hospitalized three times a week for nine months to receive aggressive chemotherapy he never gave up. Even when his hair began to fall out and his body began to waste away leaving behind only a skeletal frame he didn't give up. When the treatment and pain medication robbed him of sleep and began making him hallucinate he did not give up. When he no longer physically recognized the man he had become he did not give up.

He trusted himself and his magic and kept fighting. He made a decision every single day that his life was worth it. This is what you call intention. He was determined to create the result which he desired. Mahatma Gandhi once said,

> *"There is a force in the universe which, if we permit, will flow through us and produce miraculous results."*

That force in the universe is the same force we each have within us to transform our lives. Though we cannot see it or physically feel it if we trust in it, trust ourselves, and remain open it will work in our favor to create the desired outcome. We are all divine beings and through intention and action we can create miracles. These moments of belief and synchronicity will create outcomes that you initially did not believe were possible.

FOLLOW THE YELLOW BRICK ROAD

As a child and even now, one of my all-time favorite movies is The Wizard of Oz. When I was younger I fell in love with the characters, the vivid colors and the amazing soundtrack. My sister and I would sit glued to our Zenith television singing along to the catchy songs and recite verbatim the dialogue in the film.

As I got older and as I reconnected with my source, I started to appreciate the film on a deeper more spiritual level. Dorothy, the protagonist, finds herself lost in a foreign place and spends the duration of the film trying to find her way back home to Kansas. Throughout the film she encounters obstacles and roadblocks designed to keep her from realizing her dream of returning home. How many of us on our own journey have encountered obstacles and roadblocks designed to keep us from our dreams? As an adult, for me The Wizard of Oz has become a metaphor for life.

In the spiritual sense, as Dorothy begins to follow the yellow brick road, she discovers that ultimately what she is seeking is truth, evolution, enlightenment and purpose.

Throughout her journey she befriends the scarecrow, the tin man, and the cowardly lion who are also in search of their own purpose. Together they travel to the land of Oz in hopes the great and powerful Oz can give them what they all are searching for.

In the end, they each realize their dreams, but the main lesson of the film is to demonstrate that what we are searching for has been within us all along. It reveals how any one of us can make miracles happen in even the most difficult of circumstances just by relying on the natural gifts we have been given by God.

In the film Glinda "the good witch" tells Dorothy:

> *"You've always had the power to go back to Kansas." "I have?", replies Dorothy. "Then why didn't you tell her before?" Scarecrow demands. Because she wouldn't have believed me. She had to learn it for herself." The Tin Man leans forward and asks, "What have you learned, Dorothy?" "Well, I . . . I think that is . . . that it wasn't enough just to want to see Uncle Henry and Auntie Em . . . and that if I ever go looking for my heart's desire again, I won't look any further than my own backyard; because if it isn't here, I never really lost it to begin with."*

It wasn't until the end of her journey that Glinda informed Dorothy she had the power to get home all along. Had she told her in the beginning, Dorothy would not have learned what she needed to learn. Dorothy needed to experience what she did along the Yellow Brick Road, face the challenges she encountered, and confront her fears, in order to gain the belief that she had the power inside her the entire time. Once she came to this realization, she would never forget it.

We are all like Dorothy in search of our purpose and life is like the journey along the Yellow Brick Road. We must learn for ourselves. Truth is not given so much as it is realized. And the only way you come to realize it is by looking within.

Truth is found in your own back yard. Reality is very simple. We create our own reality. The simple universal fact is if we believe it to be so, it is. Once you tap into your power, into your magic, there is nothing you cannot do. Remember, we each own a pair of ruby shoes, that when clicked with the right intention, bring magic and goodness into our life.

Questions to ponder:

How have my choices and decisions created my reality? How can I be more aware of the choices I make in the future? How can I live a more aware and intentional life? Where is my yellow brick road taking me? How can I begin to tap into my magic?

5

EUREKA!! RECOGNIZING THE AHA! MOMENT

"Free yourself from the complexities and drama of your life. Simplify. Look within. Within ourselves we all have the gifts and talents we need to fulfill the purpose we've been blessed with."
— Steve Maraboli

Moments of awakening occur at different ages and stages of our lives. A moment of awakening can best be described as a moment of sudden realization, inspiration, insight, recognition, or comprehension. Greek polymath Archimedes referred to it as eureka! Oprah calls it your Aha! moment.

Not many of us today use the term eureka, but about 2200 years ago when Archimedes stepped into his bath and exclaimed, "Eureka" what he initially was saying was "I found it." At that moment Archimedes had discovered a solution to a problem he had been pondering for a long time. It was a moment of sudden discovery.

Information designer and author Anna Vital says, “Life can be divided up into two periods. Before you know why you are alive and after. In between there is just a single moment – the Aha! moment. One brainwave that turns a person into a person on a mission.”

When you’re on a journey of self-discovery your Aha! moment is when you realize what your purpose is. It happens so suddenly that it’s almost as if you’ve known all along.

I have spent most of my life chasing the American dream. I’m an ambitious individual who believes I can have it all. In my twenties I had visions of being a homeowner, getting married, and having children. I also envisioned myself as a successful career woman. I spent most of my twenties and some of my thirties preparing myself for all the things I envisioned. I got married, became a first time home owner, earned both Bachelor and MBA degrees, became a hospital administrator at one of New York City’s busiest healthcare facilities and had a child. By the time I was 35 I had acquired everything I said I wanted.

For a long time I believed that once I acquired these things I would feel fulfilled and that my life would be complete. Now, while I am certainly proud of my accomplishments I can’t say that I feel anymore fulfilled than I did before I accomplished them. With the exception of my daughters and husband, whom without, my life would not be the same, everything else isn’t as important to me as I once believed them to be.

Having the degree and owning the home didn’t bring passion to my life. They did not make my soul come alive. They are inanimate objects that simply make life a little more comfortable. While I am grateful for what I have accomplished during my short time here on Earth they do not define me.

I am not my degree, or my career title, or my home. I am a vibrant soul meant to serve, meant to teach, meant to encourage and support. It wasn't until the birth of my first daughter that I came to this realization. It wasn't until I held her tiny body against my chest and looked into her eyes I realized what my purpose was.

Until then, I lived a self-centered existence focusing only on my wants and desires. It was at that moment I realized I was now responsible for another human life. It was now my duty to raise a strong, confident, kind, supportive and empathetic person. I knew the only way I could do that was by being the kind of woman I want her to become.

I now had some real work to do, not for myself, but for her and for all women. It was her birth that helped me discover my purpose. It was her birth that ignited my passion for working with women and helping them discover their own passions and desires.

In April 2014, almost two years after my daughter's birth, I held my first FIERCE woman workshop. FIERCE, which is an acronym for Females, Inspiring, Empowering, Recognizing, & Cultivating Evolution encourages women to embrace their fierceness. The dictionary defines fierce as showing a heartfelt and powerful intensity. That heartfelt and powerful intensity is what I encourage women to apply to all areas of their lives.

The FIERCE Woman™ (TFW) organization's mission is to promote female empowerment by facilitating workshops, events, and creating opportunities where women network, learn from each other, inspire one another, and tap into their own dreams and visions. The FIERCE Woman™ encourages women to discover their own power and use it to help themselves and their communities.

It is when I am doing TFW work I feel most fulfilled. It is when my soul comes alive and gets excited. FIERCE Woman work doesn't seem like work to me because I love doing it. I am passionate about it. It has been said that when you love what you do you'll never work a day in your life. There is some truth to that. Work won't feel like work when you enjoy doing it. The reason people often complain about their jobs is because they don't love what they do. Don't be a person who settles. Do what you have to do so you can eventually do what you want.

In a 2005 Stanford commencement speech, Steve Jobs summarized his guiding principle in life in his talk titled "How to Live Before You Die". He said,

> *"You've got to find what you love. And that is as true for your work as it is for your lovers. Your work is going to fill a large part of your life, and the only way to be truly satisfied is to do what you believe is great work. And the only way to do great work is to love what you do. If you haven't found it yet, keep looking. Don't settle. As with all matters of the heart, you'll know when you find it. And, like any great relationship, it just gets better and better as the years roll on. So keep looking. Don't settle."*

The work I do to help empower women is evolving. I now have created an extension of TFW for young girls, appropriately called FIERCE Girls.

As a mother of two girls and the aunt of two teen nieces I realized when you empower girls at an early age the confidence they develop follows them into adulthood. It's why I believe FIERCE girls become FIERCE women.

Part of my life's purpose is to provide the young women in my life the tools necessary to help them become strong, confident, fearless women. As I help them discover their own magic I am also compelled to help other young girls discover theirs. Empowering and inspiring others is what drives me. Every morning in my prayers I ask God to use me in whatever way is necessary. I am here to be of service. That is my purpose.

If you haven't discovered your purpose or had your own aha! moment yet then try to think about a time when you felt most fulfilled. Think about what you were doing and why you were doing it. Think about a time when you felt like the best version of yourself. Though the activities themselves may be different there may be a common thread. Pay attention to it because those things are tied to what makes your soul come alive. Whatever it is that excites you will be part of an overarching theme that will help you learn how to discover your passion in life.

Passion and purpose are not about being happy or blissful every day of your life, but instead are about what you are willing to suffer for. They are the things you are willing to sacrifice and give your all for. When you are passionate about what you do not only are you more invested, but you also become more fulfilled. Some discover their purpose early on in life and others discover it over time.

If you have not found your purpose yet, don't worry. When you do recognize it, it will come at the right time and when it does you will be ready!

Questions to ponder:

What things do I enjoy doing? What excites me right now? What things make me feel most alive? What are my superpowers (what are my powers and strengths)? How can I make a living from doing the things I enjoy?

6

CREATE THE VISION

"Write the vision, make it plain."
Habakkuk 2 New King James Version (NKJV)

In January 2011 I attended a spiritual retreat that absolutely changed the direction of my life. I was at a crossroads and I wasn't sure what I wanted to do with myself. I was feeling unhappy, uncertain, doubtful, and empty. Despite having a great career, a loving husband, a beautiful home, and loving family I felt like something was missing, but I wasn't sure what it was.

So, when a friend invited me to attend this one day spiritual retreat described as a *workshop where women gather in sacred space to release, forgive and let go of the old, and create new visions, desires, and goals*, I said to myself *"Why not?"* I figured this was exactly what I needed to help me get rid of all the negative feelings and energy I had been feeling. Even if it didn't work, it couldn't make things any worse.

The morning of the retreat I arrived not knowing what to expect. I was hopeful the retreat, which focused on *spiritual cleansing and healing for the soul,* would provide me with the spiritual rejuvenation I needed to get myself back on track with the dreams I'd always envisioned for myself. I kept an open mind and an open heart and when I arrived what awaited me was a room full of women who each had the same intention, *"It's time to take care of me."*

There were approximately 12 to 14 women in attendance, all with a desire to reclaim the parts of themselves they had lost or felt were missing. Women who all had something they wanted to release and let go in order to get back to their essence. We cramped into the small one bedroom Harlem apartment that was the location of the day long retreat. We spent the day journaling, meditating, and self-reflecting. At one point the facilitator asked each of us what our heart's deepest desire was. She gave us time to sit and meditate on it. She asked us to quiet our minds and pay special attention to any images, sounds, smells, colors, and visions that came to mind.

My deepest desire was to be a mother. I wanted to be a mother for a very long time and despite my efforts it hadn't happened. I gave up on that dream because I started believing since it hadn't happened in ten years then it probably wasn't meant to be. During the exercise I refused to revisit that dream and instead convinced myself that my deepest desire was to complete my book manuscript and get it published.

After a few minutes of meditating she paired us up in groups of two and for three minutes we had to share with our partner our deepest desire. You know what they say about speaking it into existence? That was what the exercise was designed to do. I was paired with a beautiful curly haired woman who had never done any spiritual work either. We agreed she would share first. We sat Indian style with our legs crossed and faced each other. She began to speak and as I watched her lips move my ears could not believe what they were hearing. "My deepest desire for 2011 is to have a baby", she said.

My heart felt like it was going to explode through my chest. I felt sweat beads begin to form in the palms of my hands and despite my will to control my tears they fell anyway. As she continued speaking, I could no longer control my emotions and began crying. By the confused look on her face I could tell she was wondering why her deepest desire was making me cry.

That experience was the biggest and clearest sign from God telling me not to give up on my desire to be a mother. I couldn't pretend anymore. I couldn't hide behind the excuses I convinced myself to believe. My deepest desire was staring me in the face in the form of this beautiful woman. She was my mirror and I was forced to look at her. She was saying to me all of the things I felt and for so long had tried to deny.

It proved to me that our pairing up was no coincidence. It was the Universe telling me loud and clear not to give up on my dream of becoming a mother. After we each shared and during one of the many journaling exercises that day I finally wrote the following:

My deepest desire for 2011 is to become a mother
by whatever means that happens.

That day I decided I was no longer going to deny what my heart wanted most and began the year long self-work with the *DeAlmas Women's Institute* that helped me rediscover my dreams. What started out as a one day workshop turned into a yearlong commitment to working on myself.

Through meditation, self-reflection, journaling, sister-sharing and visioning I was able to tap back into my spirit and nourish it with what it was missing. Love. Somewhere along my journey through life I stopped loving myself like I should have.

During my spiritual journey I realized I had spent so much time trying to please others I had neglected my own goals, desires, and dreams. The retreat and the subsequent self-work I did in 2011 helped me realign myself with my heart's deepest desires. It forced me to acknowledge a dream I had convinced myself I did not want.

For a very long time I wanted to have children, but my inability to conceive, up to that point, had made me bitter and unhappy. I chose to bury that dream in the deepest parts of me believing if I ignored it or didn't think about it the desire would eventually go away. It didn't. Instead, it resulted in me being resentful, jealous, and miserable. How many of us are guilty of doing this? How many of us convince ourselves that our dreams are not worth pursuing because *it's too hard*, or *seems impossible*?

Once I let go of those negative feelings and started truly believing in my own God-like power to manifest my dreams my entire outlook on life changed. I started to believe in my own magic and the *change your thoughts, change your life* concept was something I actively worked on cultivating. Whenever a negative thought entered my mind I immediately shut it down and changed it into something positive and affirming.

Additionally, I started a journaling practice and began journaling every day. I wrote down every dream, goal, and vision I had. I began meditating. I learned how to sit with myself in silence and listen to my inner voice.

One time in particular, as part of a take home exercise from my self-work with DeAlmas I was instructed by the facilitator to go home, find a quiet space, meditate and pay special attention to sounds, smells, images, visions, feelings and whatever popped into my head. After I meditated I was then supposed to write a letter to myself as if it was the end of the year. The facilitator wanted me to envision what my life would look like at the end of the self-work journey. This exercise was the first time I had ever truly written down my vision. The Bible says,

> *"Write the vision and make it plain on tablets, that he may run who reads it. For the vision is yet for an appointed time; But at the end it will speak, and it will not lie.*
> *Though it tarries, wait for it;*
> *Because it will surely come,*
> *It will not tarry."- Habakkuk 2 New King James Version (NKJV)*

After lighting candles and finding a comfortable spot on the floor in my home office I cleared my mind and began meditating. So many things came up for me during that meditation. There were images of the ocean, the beach, a tropical breeze, the number five, the color white, feelings of happiness and joy, warmth, the sun, and an overwhelming sense of peace.

When my mediation was done I began journaling making sure to pay attention to all that had presented itself during the meditation. I didn't think about it, I simply picked up my pen and started writing a letter to myself as if it was already December 2011.

Below is an excerpt from the journal entry:

April 6, 2011

Dear Nancy,

This has been an amazing year for you. You set yourself on a path of creation and create you did. This year you gave life to Nancy, the spoken word performer. You completed and published your first book of poetry and short stories and gave life to Nancy, the author. As the waves crash against the shore as you take it all in, the warmth of the sun coddles me. You look beautiful in your white flowing summer dress as it sits right below your knees and you embrace the sand with your toes.

I know it took a lot of soul searching and spiritual growth but you let go of your doubts, fears, procrastination, and all of the resentment you harbored and opened yourself up to the blessing that is me.

I am five months now. I can hardly believe it myself. Why did you envision me at five months? Do you know how divine that number is? It is not a coincidence that the number five is the number that came to mind as you thought of me in my fifth month in the womb.

Five is the number associated with Oshun, the goddess of prosperity and fertility. She is the cool water that heals the sick abdomen and brings children to the barren. It is said she provides renewal when no one else can and know that with me you are renewed.

This has been a long journey for the both of us, but this is only the beginning. So mother, I tell you bask in it. Rejoice in it. Be thankful for it and just promise to love me the way I already love you.

Signed, Your Unborn Child

It's been five years (there goes that number five again) since I wrote that or even looked at it and when I wrote it I had no idea I was manifesting my heart's deepest desire. *Write the vision, make it plain.* At the time I had no clue what the significance of the number five was. I am not a follower of the Lucumi religion, but back then I was praying to every God, *orisha*, saint, and goddess and Oshun being the goddess of fertility was one of them.

Looking back, I now know the significance of the number five. The number five is associated with Oshun. May is the fifth month of the year and it is also my birth month. In May 2011 I conceived for the first time ever. Unfortunately that pregnancy resulted in a miscarriage, but five months later in November 2011 I conceived again. My oldest daughter was born July 2012. If you follow numerology you will see that the year 2012, when the numbers are added up is equal to five.

My daughter is now four years old, happy healthy, and a big sister. There are signs all around us designed to lead us towards our destiny. You just have to learn how to recognize them and pay attention to them.

> *"Keep in mind this basic axiom—if all that now exists was once imagined, then what you want to exist for you in the future must now be imagined."*
> *— Wayne W. Dyer, Wishes Fulfilled: Mastering the Art of Manifesting*

Every single thing I wrote in that letter manifested itself by December 2011. Since then I am an advocate of writing the vision. It is why I create a vision board at the beginning of every year and the reason I write down every single dream, vision, and goal I want to accomplish. I don't concern myself with the *how*. I simply write it down knowing and believing that if I work hard, stay focused and committed the *how* will take care of itself.

> *"The first step toward creating an improved future is developing the ability to envision it. VISION will ignite the fire of passion that fuels our commitment to do whatever it takes to achieve excellence. Only*

VISION allows us to transform dreams of greatness into the reality of achievement through human action. VISION has no boundaries and knows no limits. Our VISION is what we become in life. "
— Tony Dungy

It all starts with a vision. You have to see yourself doing it then tell yourself "I can" and "I will". Believing you can is the first step to success. Create a big vision. Once you do, all these doors you didn't even know existed will start to open.

Questions to ponder:

What dreams have I given up on? If money, time, fear, or risk weren't factors what would I do? If I could do or be anything I would do ___________ or be ___________________. My heart's deepest desire is ____________________ (fill in the blanks).

**Develop a journaling practice and start writing down all your dreams, goals, and visions. Write the vision, make it plain.*

7

BELIEVING IS HALF THE BATTLE

"If you believe it, if you can see it, if you act from it, it will show up for you." – Michael Beckwith

---

One of the greatest obstacles in fulfilling our dreams is overcoming the idea that our dreams are impossible to achieve. This type of negative thinking is a sure fire way to limit our potential and it keeps us stuck in day to day monotonous living. It's the sort of thinking that steals our joy and robs us of our passions. Yet, so many live their lives believing they will never amount to more than their current situation. Not realizing that if they shifted their thinking from *I can't* to *I can* the possibilities would be limitless.

Believing in ourselves doesn't necessarily mean we have all the answers when we start. It is very likely we won't. We may not even know where to begin or have the resources or finances to support our dreams. That's not what believing in ourselves is.

Believing in ourselves means that even though we may have no clue how we will accomplish our goals, we trust ourselves, our talents, and our God given abilities enough to try; knowing that as long as we try and don't give up, success is inevitable.

Many of us are familiar with the story of *The Little Engine That Could*. The story of the little engine has been told and retold many times. The underlying theme is the same — a stranded train is unable to find an engine willing to take it over the mountain to its destination. Only the little blue engine is willing to try and, while repeating the mantra "I think I can, I think I can", eventually does. The story of the little engine is just one example of how what we tell ourselves influences our belief in ourselves. By affirming *I can,* we are affirming our power as creators knowing that we indeed can accomplish our goals as long as we are willing to try. The single greatest thing we can do to achieve success is to change our inner voice.

Our words become our reality. You have to prophesize your future. When you get your words going in the right direction your life will go in the right direction. You have to get in the habit of speaking your dreams into existence. Not only speak it, but see it as if they have already happened. When you believe, it is only a matter of time before your reality catches up with your vision.

The main difference I've observed between successful people and unsuccessful people isn't intelligence or opportunity or resources. It's believing our goals are impossible to accomplish.

Failure and uncertainty is common and when your pursuing your dreams the closer you get to realizing them, the more obstacles you're going to encounter.

The person who ultimately succeeds is the person who never gives up. It's the person who despite not having all the answers, ventures forward trusting they will discover the solution along the way. It's amazing the things we can accomplish when we don't give up.

In early 2008, after years of renting various apartments throughout New York City, my husband and I decided we wanted to purchase a home. We both had stable jobs and felt it was time. The house hunting process was exhausting and grueling.

First, we had to look at our finances and decide what we realistically could afford to buy. We then had to decide on the location where we wanted to buy a home. Several things factored into location. For starters we wanted a low crime area. It had to be close to public transportation and no more than an hour commute to my job in Manhattan and property taxes had to be reasonable. After setting a budget, choosing a location, and finding a realtor we began looking at houses.

We must have looked at hundreds of houses. If we loved them, they weren't within our budget. If they were within the range of what we could afford they were old, dilapidated, and needed tons of work. When we finally found one that we loved and was affordable the couple decided to take it off the market and we were right back where we started.

It was an arduous experience and there were many times I felt like we would never find the house of our dreams. Till one day our realtor informed us of a house she thought would be perfect for us.

It had just been put on the market and the owners were looking to sell quickly.

On a sunny Saturday afternoon my husband and I drove from our Bronx apartment into New Jersey to take a look at the house. It was an open house and we arrived early. We parked in front of the house while we waited for our realtor to arrive. From the outside it looked absolutely perfect. It sat on the corner of a tree lined street with a nice sized perfectly manicured lawn. The owners obviously took good care of the property. Fresh mulch had been laid and flowers were beginning to grow along the side of the house. The enclosed porch was decorated with beautiful hanging plants. From the outside, the house was perfect.

When our realtor arrived and we finally had the opportunity to walk through the house I immediately fell in love. It was everything we wanted and it was within our budget. My husband and I put in an offer immediately. Our offer was accepted, but that was just the beginning. Though we had been pre-approved by a mortgage lender, after running our finances which included my outstanding student loan debt, our mortgage broker informed us it was possible we wouldn't be approved for a loan. He said even if we were approved, based on our income and all the additional expenses that come with owning a house we would eventually default.

I remember going home that evening and sitting in the bedroom of our Bronx apartment crying and feeling defeated. After all the houses we looked at and all the time spent filling out paper work I felt like my dream of becoming a homeowner was not going to happen. I had even begun regretting my decision to pursue a graduate degree which was what added to my student loan debt. I figured if I hadn't pursued a master's degree I would have never taken out the additional student loans. It was one of the lowest points in my life. I felt like such a failure.

My husband noticing my sadness and defeated attitude refused to allow me to sulk and give in to the negative feelings I was feeling. He gave me a pep talk and reminded me that if this house was indeed meant for us nothing could or would stand in our way of having it.

We ran the numbers and based on our calculations we could afford the house. This was the house we wanted and after the pep talk he had given me, I shifted my thinking. I let go of the words spoken to us by the realtor and started believing that this house was indeed our house.

I believed it so much that I began telling family members and friends we purchased the home even before we had actually bought it. I began visualizing all the things I would do in our new home. I started looking at furniture advertisements because I knew it was just a matter of time until my reality caught up with my visions.

Our loan eventually got approved and as if that wasn't exciting enough, one week before our closing date I started a new job earning twenty thousand dollars more than my previous job. Where we once were crunching numbers trying to figure out if we could afford the additional debt we were now reveling in this blessing and thanking God for this windfall.

Not only did God give us the house we so badly wanted the Universe also made sure that we were in a good position financially to meet our new debt obligations. Since then my household income has steadily increased each year and in the eight years since we purchased our home we have not missed one mortgage payment.

> *Believe in your ability to be successful in the things you have a passion for. These are God given gifts for you to use. -Catherine Pulsifer*

One of the most important lessons I've learned is we have the power to create our reality by the kind of thoughts we have. If you think you can, you will. If you think you can't, you won't. Don't talk yourself out of your dreams before even trying.

Believe in your dreams enough to at least take a chance on yourself. When you want something bad enough, let that drive push you to make it happen. You don't have to know how it's going to happen just believe it will. This is the attitude I apply to everything in my life.

I am constantly setting new goals and dreams for myself. Half the time I have no idea how I'm going to accomplish them, but I don't allow myself to worry about the how. I focus my time and energy doing the work. When you do the work somehow and some way the doors open and the opportunities show up.

Believing in your talents and God given gifts is a scary thing. It requires letting go of fear and letting go the idea that we are not good enough; the idea that we don't deserve greatness. Sometimes you'll run into brick walls (or mortgage brokers) that are put there to test you, to test your commitment, and to test how bad you really want it. Don't let the brick walls stop you. Find a way through them. If you can't find a way through them then find a way around them. If you can't find a way around them then find a way to knock them down. Always stay focused on your dream. Success is inevitable for the person who doesn't quit.

There are a lot of ways you can fail at something. There are few ways you can succeed at anything. But one thing is for sure, if you do not believe you can succeed to the core of your body, then you will never succeed. Believing you can achieve something is the very first step you need to take on the road to success.

Questions to ponder:

What beliefs about myself prevent me from realizing my dreams? What things, words, or thoughts prevent me from believing in myself? What steps/actions can I take to overcome this?

8

YOU GOTTA DO THE WORK

"No action steps, no action, no results. The actual outcome of any idea is dependent on the action steps that are taken and completed by you."

I often say the only thing greater than my ambition is my hustle. Having a vision or a great idea isn't enough. We have to actively work towards making that vision a reality if we want to see results. From the microwaves we use to heat our foods, to our laptops, to our smart phones, even the internet and social media every great invention started as a dream, a thought, a vision. All of them were once just a thought in someone's mind.

Where did all these inventions come from? What was it that took the idea and turned it into something useful and tangible? The answer is simple. Each inventor did the work. From creating a prototype to obtaining a patent to getting it on the market all of that requires work and without rolling up your sleeves and actually working, your idea will remain an idea.

I can't begin to tell you how many emails I receive from individuals inquiring about how to get started writing a book. They don't ask me about the actual writing process, but instead are more concerned with the publishing process and how to get their book out to the public. When I ask if they've completed their manuscript, 99 percent of them haven't even started. I tell them to get back to me once they've actually written something.

Contrary to what some may think writing is more than putting words to paper. Writing, like any other art form, requires practice. Which is to say you're not going to be great your first go round. You have to invest in your writing craft like you would anything else. You have to put in the work.

I tell them to take writing classes to learn about voice, plot, tension, and developing characters. If they aren't already writing voraciously I tell them to start a journal or a blog and to write as much as possible. I tell them to share their work with writers they respect for honest feedback and critique. Many want the recognition and fame without putting in the sweat and tears. And while writing a book has its appeal, in order to be taken seriously as a writer and be respected, you have to be willing to get your hands dirty.

A couple of years ago I met a young Hispanic woman by the name of Raygrid Calderon who attended one of my FIERCE

Woman events. She is a self-taught coder and had a vision of developing an app that created opportunities for up-and-coming businesses and innovators looking for business placement to connect with potential employees and candidates for partnerships.

Not knowing a thing about coding or how to develop an app, Raygrid credits books she purchased at Barnes & Noble and countless hours spent watching YouTube as her initial teachers. The app originally launched in 2013 and in July 2016 she re-launched the app with more features and functionality. Since its creation the app has helped start over a dozen startups, inspired and motivated entrepreneurs, and has been recognized by big outside companies such as Sprite.

What impressed me most when I first met her was her determination, passion, and belief in herself and her idea. She believed in herself so much that she is self-funded and because she is investing her own money, she is even more committed to winning and succeeding. She realizes as a Latina woman in tech, which is a highly male dominated industry, she has to work twice as hard, speak twice as loud, and make her presence a little more felt in order to be recognized and respected. While some sit back and wait for handouts or wait for someone to discover them this young woman is actively making her dreams come true.

You can't wait for some miracle to change your life. In order for miracles to happen we have to actively participate in the manifestation of miracles. It isn't enough to just wish our dreams into reality. We create miracles when we have a clear vision, a positive outlook, and make moves. Action is what makes miracles happen.

How exactly do we do that? By being active participants in the creation of the idea; by strategizing, visualizing, planning, and executing. When you contribute to making things happen, they eventually happen, sometimes quite fast, and sometimes, gradually, over a period of time. Either way, nothing ever comes into fruition without actively working towards it.

TURNING DREAMS INTO GOALS

I am a huge advocate and user of vision boards. Every January I make a list of my dreams. Sometimes my dreams are big and outrageous and other times they are simple. Regardless of which category they fall into I always break each dream down into goals. Why? Because a dream without a plan is a fantasy and I am not in the business of wasting my time on fantasies.

When we take the time to look at our dreams and break them down into goals what we are doing is setting the foundation for that dream to come into fruition. A goal is something we want bad enough that we make an effort to reach it. It is a desired result a person envisions, plans, and commits to achieving. A goal is not the same as a want.

For example, a person might want a nicer car than the one she can currently afford to own, but it's not really one of her goals. Wanting a nicer car in that case is more like a fantasy. It's something a person might like to think about from time to time, but has no intention of trying to get. We can imagine what it's like to drive around in a nicer car than the one we have. We can imagine a smoother ride; imagine our friends being impressed with our beautiful and fancy new car, but unless we want that car enough to work at getting it, it will remain a fantasy, not a goal. A dream could be a fantasy or a goal. For example, there are times when I dream about winning the lotto. Maybe you have too. I imagine what I would do with the money. I fantasize about the exotic places I'd visit, the mansion I'd buy, about how much I'd invest and how much I'd donate to charity. I think about how significantly my life would change if I won. The only problem is I don't play the lotto. So, while it is a dream, in this instance it is more of a fantasy because I am not doing anything to make that dream come true. You can't win if you don't play.

When we want something, we often call it our dream, but without action that dream can never materialize. Take Beyoncé, Oprah, or Jennifer Lopez, for instance, each one of these women are each at the top of their industry. They never would have achieved their dreams by sitting back and doing nothing. Each one had to work very hard, for years, to make their dreams come true. They set goals and then created a plan to achieve them.

I have plenty of dreams, some of which I've already accomplished. Each one required me to work hard and at times push myself passed my limits. When you apply yourself and learn how to get out of your own way, success becomes inevitable. Sometimes the main obstacle to accomplishing our goals is ourselves. When we stop being our own worst enemy and start believing in ourselves our reality starts to change. The boulder that once seemed immovable slowly turns into a pebble. That door that once seemed dead bolted suddenly opens up.

> *You don't have enough faith," Jesus told them. "I tell you the truth, if you had faith even as small as a mustard seed, you could say to this mountain,*

'Move from here to there,' and it would move. Nothing would be impossible."- Matthew 17:20, New Living Translation

We can wish and want and pray for our dreams to come true, but no matter how much we may want something and no matter how much fun it is to think about dreams, they are not goals until we are prepared to work on turning them into reality. Part of that work requires us to believe more than anything our dream is possible. When we set goals we are telling the Universe we are prepared to do whatever it takes to accomplish them. Why are setting goals important? Because goals are the roadmap to achieving your dreams. The process of setting goals helps you choose where you want to go in life. By knowing precisely what you want to achieve, you know where you have to concentrate your efforts. You'll also quickly spot the distractions that can, so easily, lead you astray.

Without setting clear, measurable goals you won't be able to assess your progress or refocus should you lose momentum. Goals help to keep you on track while simultaneously motivating you as you complete each goal and begin tackling the next one. When you visualize, affirm, believe, and act the Universe has a way of giving you exactly what you dreamed of.

Questions to ponder:

How are you making the most out of your time? What tools do you use to keep you focused and motivated on your goals? What unproductive things can you begin cutting out of your day so that you can re-allocate that time working on your goals?

9

LIVING YOUR PURPOSE

"There is no greater gift you can give or receive than to honor your calling. It's why you were born. And how you become most truly alive."
— Oprah Winfrey

Oprah Winfrey or Aunty Oprah as she's known in my head, is one of my greatest inspirations. When I think about the kind of life I want to live I often use Oprah as a reference. Not because of her incredible fame and fortune (though that is a perk), but because she, for me, represents someone who is truly living in her purpose. Not only is she the Queen of all media, she has been ranked the richest African-American of the 20th century, the greatest black philanthropist in American history, and is currently North America's first and only multi-billionaire black person. To me, she is the representation of the American Dream. She personifies the saying "Started from the bottom, now we here."

From being born into poverty to being a rape survivor, to creating one of the most successful media empires Oprah's life is a testament to what beating the odds looks like. She has never allowed any obstacle, struggle, or roadblock to stop her from living her life's purpose. She's used every opportunity and every setback as a guide to fulfilling her life's purpose.

> *I've come to believe that each of us has a personal calling that's as unique as a fingerprint – and that the best way to succeed is to discover what you love and then find a way to offer it to others in the form of service, working hard, and also allowing the energy of the universe to lead you. – Oprah Winfrey*

Almost every person who has had even a modicum of success says doing what you love is the key to personal fulfillment and success. Imagine living a life you don't need a vacation from. Imagine waking up every morning and wanting to go to work. Imagine looking forward to Monday with the same enthusiasm, passion, and excitement as you do Friday afternoon. That is what living your purpose does for you. It's being in love with every second of your life, even when it gets difficult. It's knowing and trusting the Universe has placed you exactly where you need to be doing exactly what you were meant to do.

During a talk at the Stanford Graduate School of Business in April 2014 Oprah told the crowd, "The truth is I have from the very beginning listened to my instincts. All of my best decisions in life have come because I was attuned to what really felt like the next right move for me…

...Knowing what you don't want to do is the best possible place to be if you don't know what to do, because knowing what you don't want to do leads you to figure out what it is you really want." We have to let go of the belief that we must know the direction our life has to take at all times. We don't. It's OK if you don't know what your purpose is right now, or where the next step on your life's journey will be. Sometimes that space of unknowing is exactly where you need to be. It is during those times of uncertainty that we are challenged to really look at ourselves and push ourselves harder than ever before. It is our opportunity to do a self-assessment and acknowledge whether or not we are truly fulfilled and happy.

If you find that you are at a point in your life where you are feeling unfulfilled, unsatisfied, or feel like a hamster chasing the hamster wheel don't be too hard on yourself. The fact you can acknowledge this is the first step in making a change. You can't change what you don't know exists.

Take inventory of your life and of the things that are contributing to those unfulfilling feelings. Simultaneously think about what it is that makes you feel most fulfilled. Maybe it's writing or baking or decorating, but whatever it is, think about the things you most enjoy doing, the things that make you feel good and most fulfilled. Pay attention to what they are because those are the things you are most passionate about. Revered T.D. Jakes said it best,

> *"If you can't figure out your purpose, figure out your passion. For your passion will lead you right into your purpose."*

Living in your purpose has less to do with how much money you earn and more to do with the impact your work and your life is making in the lives of others and on the Universe overall. We are all parts of a larger puzzle that when put together impacts the world on a global level.

What we do or don't do matters. Our actions, experiences, and lives creates our legacy. It is what we leave our children and our children's children. It is what we leave to the world. What you do matters. Your life matters. That's why it's important to figure out what it is you love and devote every second of your life to doing it.

Take Steve Jobs for example. He is only one person, but his life significantly changed the way the world communicates. Through his vision, passion, and love for his job Steve Jobs made Apple the most valuable company in history. How did he do it? Simply by listening to his heart. He spent every day of his life doing what he loved.

> *I'm convinced that the only thing that kept me going was that I loved what I did. You've got to find what you love... Your work is going to fill a large part of your life, and the only way to be truly satisfied is to do what you believe is great work. And the only way to do great work is to love what you do... Don't let the noise of others' opinions drown out your own inner voice. And most important, have the courage to follow your heart and intuition. They somehow already know what you truly want to become.- Steve Jobs*

Follow your heart and intuition. It's the simplest yet greatest thing you can ever do. Though it can be scary to follow our hearts, what's scarier is living a mediocre life. You were not meant to live a mediocre life. You were created to live the best, greatest, most fulfilling life you can imagine for yourself. Living a mediocre is not your destiny. You were destined for greatness. Repeat this to yourself.

I am destined for greatness.

Every morning when you wake up look in the mirror and say that to yourself. Every night before you close your eyes repeat it. Repeat it over and over and over until that belief becomes a part of you because we become that which we affirm about ourselves.

It is important to remember you were intentionally created by the Creator. Your life is not a mistake. You are not a mistake. Regardless of the mistakes you may have made in your life, you are not your mistakes. It is how you move forward and push passed them that matters. It may very well be your mistakes are the very things that will put you on the path of your purpose. Therefore, being able to discern the act that led to the mistake from the lesson it was designed to teach is essential. The lessons learned from those mistakes may serve as a tool to help others.

Your duty in life is to discover what's the contribution you are called to give to the world. To look at yourself and ask yourself "What purpose am I serving with my life?" I encourage you to write those words down. Say them out loud. Meditate on them and then wait to see how the answer is revealed to you. It may come in the form of a thought, or in a song, or in a street sign, or in a scent. The key is to remain open and to pay attention to the signs in whatever way they present themselves. The answer may come quickly or it may take some time.

Whichever way the answer is revealed is not important. What is important is what you do once it is. What actions will you take?

How will you restructure your life so that you are living more intentionally and more purposefully?

Your real work is to figure out your strengths, talents (both God given and learned) and align them with your personality and your humanitarian duty to be of service. When you align your personality with your purpose you become unstoppable.

Questions to ponder:

What activities do you most enjoying doing? What things bring you the most joy and happiness? What causes/issues are you most passionate about? Think of a time where you were truly happy. What were you doing? Who were you with? What do you need to do to or what steps do you need to take to recreate that experience?

A GUIDE ON HOW TO LIVE A PURPOSEFUL AND EMPOWERED LIFE

THE WORKBOOK

Learning to Live On Purpose
A Note From the Author

To realize one's purpose in life is one of the most exciting and fulfilling revelations one can discover. Yet, there are many that have no clue what their life's purpose is and are even less clear on how to go about figuring it out. The questions on the following pages have been designed as a way to do a little self-inventory and to get you thinking about what your life's purpose is.

The goal is that as you work through the questions you think about those things that most inspire, motivate, and excite you. You may start to see a pattern as you start writing down your answers. Pay attention to the patterns. Consider how your answers are influenced by your experiences. Hopefully, as you begin to identify the things you are most passionate about a spark will be ignited and that spark will light your soul on fire with purpose.

~Nancy Arroyo Ruffin~

Explore

When you were a child what did you want to be when you grew up? What qualities or characteristics attracted you to those roles?

What's been most meaningful to you in life? List some of your most meaningful experiences and explain why they were so important to you. What made them so significant.

What has your life experience told you about your destiny?

Where do you find your bliss? What brings you the most joy?

What would you do if money and fear weren't factors?

What issues or causes do you care about most in the world around you? How do they influence the way you live your life? ❤

What are you most afraid of? What actions/steps can you take to overcome your fear?

What do you really, really want? What are you willing to sacrifice in order to get it?

Visualize

What dream do you envision for your life (career, finances, family, health, self-growth, helping others)?

What is the essence of that dream? What makes you want to live it, no matter what?

What experiences do you want to have in your lifetime?

What do you want to create in your lifetime?

What will you miss out on if you don't take a chance on your dreams? What will you gain if you do?

Pretend it's 10 years into the future. When you are older and look back on your life what do you see? Write a letter to your present day self about what your future looks like and all you've accomplished. When you're done, place that letter somewhere you can see it every day, as a reminder of the work you have ahead of you, to make sure your future is as you described in the letter.

Take Action

What steps do you have to take in order to turn your dream into reality? Identify any potential obstacles and solutions. Establish timeframes.

What other resources can you tap into?

Heart Gem Reflection

Now that you've explored your heart and answered the heart gems related to the things you're passionate and care most about, identify any themes. Are there any similarities in your answers? Is there a pattern developing between the things you care most about and the things that bring you the most joy? If so, what are they? What do these things inspire you to do? How can you incorporate more of these experiences into your daily life? What steps must you take?

If you find it difficult to identify themes or similarities take a few minutes to meditate on your responses to the questions. It may be possible there aren't any obvious similarities, but just because they aren't obvious doesn't mean there aren't any. All it means is you have to dig deeper. Find a comfortable and quiet space to meditate and then ask yourself why you answered the questions the way you did. What factors influenced your replies? What feelings do your answers stir up in you? What images appear to you when you think about your answers to the questions? What is your inner voice saying to you?

Sit in silence for as long as you need to until the answer reveals itself to you. It may come in the form of a sound, or a smell, or a sensation in your body. Whatever it is pay attention to it. Write it down in your journal.

Embrace God's Plan For Your Life

The journey to self-discovery is not an easy one. It requires patience, a willingness to relinquish control, and remaining open to what the Universe has in store. Trusting that every experience, whether positive or negative, is for your greater good.

The concept of giving up control is a scary one for many especially if you are a person who is used to always being in control. When trying to discover your purpose you have to let go and let God. What does that mean? It means that instead of being driven by ego, which is the conscious part of our personality, you allow your intuition, your heart, take the wheel.

Our egos are motivated by the world around us. The ego separates out what is real and helps us to organize our thoughts and make sense of them. The ego is directly influenced by the external world and represents what may be called reason and common sense. In order to tap into who we truly are we have to relinquish the ego and get in tune with our subconscious. This is where our passions reside. When trying to discover our purpose and what we were put on this Earth to do the last thing you want is to be limited by reason and common sense. Sometimes who we are destined to be doesn't make sense to the average person and it doesn't have to.

Take the story of the Virgin Mary for instance. Jesus was conceived through immaculate conception. Now, for the average person it seems like an impossible feat. It doesn't make sense because it goes against everything we've learned about conception. Yet, this is how Jesus came into the world. When we can let go of others' expectations of us and the desire to fit in we begin to construct a new vision for ourselves and our lives.

The questions in the preceding pages were designed to help you tap back into your essence. Your essence is the core of who you are. It's your spirit. It's your soul. It is the part of you that you were born with and the part of your being that you've carried with you through birth, childhood, your teenage years, and into adulthood. It is the part of you that has remained unchanged even though your physical body has changed many times.

Learning to tap into your unconsciousness and listening to your intuition is the beginning of the self-discovery process. When you allow yourself to listen to that part of you and to make decisions from that place of unconsciousness you will soon find that your purpose will be revealed to you. And when it is, it will feel like a spiritual awakening. The more you live in your purpose the more happiness, joy, and peace will consume you.

It is never too late to discover your purpose. Living the life you've always dreamed of is your duty. In the words of the great Sufi poet Jalaluddin Rumi, "And you? When will you begin that long journey into yourself?"

Connect with Nancy on Social Media at:

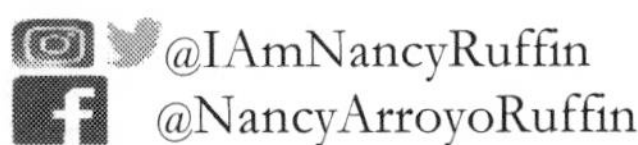

@IAmNancyRuffin
@NancyArroyoRuffin

Or visit her website for more info:
www.nancyarroyoruffin.com
www.thefiercewoman.com

For bookings or readings email:
info@nancyarroyoruffin.com

Also by Nancy Arroyo Ruffin

ABOUT THE AUTHOR

Nancy Arroyo Ruffin is a mother, wife, award winning writer, on-line radio talk show host, empowerment speaker and social media influencer. Nancy describes herself as the offspring of Biggie and Deepak (Chopra) because of her Brooklyn girl attitude and Zen spirituality. This combination makes Nancy a highly sought out speaker because of her ability to connect well with diverse audiences.

Nancy is the co-host of the popular on-line weekly podcast The EmpowHERment Hour: Where pop culture and feminism intersect. In the hour long broadcast, Nancy brings her unique perspective on pop culture, current events, and social issues as viewed through a feminist lens. Her written work has been cited and published in various online magazines and literary journals such as Duende, The Elephant Journal, CENTRO Voices, Poets & Writers, The Huffington Post, For Harriet, Mutha Magazine, & Latin Trends magazine among others.

Nancy is the recipient of the Blogher 2016 Voices of the Year Award, she is a 2014 VONA Fellow and the 2014 International Latino Book Award recipient for her sophomore collection of poetry Letters to My Daughter (CreativeInk Press, 2013). Live on Purpose is her fourth published book and she chronicles her work, which primarily centers around culture, feminism, and motherhood on her personal blog www.nancyruffin.com.

78555749R00112

Made in the USA
Columbia, SC
17 October 2017